W9-APD-601

American Lives

Julia Ward Howe

Elizabeth Raum

Heinemann Library
Chicago, Illinois

© 2004 Heinemann Library
a division of Reed Elsevier Inc.
Chicago, Illinois

Customer Service 888-454-2279

Visit our website at www.heinemannlibrary.com

All rights reserved. No part of this publication may
be reproduced or transmitted in any form or by any
means, electronic or mechanical, including
photocopying, recording, taping, or any information
storage and retrieval system, without permission in
writing from the publisher.

Designed by Heinemann Library
Photo research by Eva Schorr
Printed in China by WKT Company Limited.

08 07 06 05 04
10 9 8 7 6 5 4 3 2 1

Library of Congress Cataloging-in-Publication Data
Raum, Elizabeth.
  Julia Ward Howe / Elizabeth Raum.
    p. cm. -- (American lives)
Summary: A biography of the nineteenth century
woman known for writing the poem that became
"The Battle Hymn of the Republic" and for her work
against slavery and for the cause of women getting
the right to vote.
Includes bibliographical references (p.   ) and index.
  ISBN 1-4034-4995-3 (Hardcover) --
  ISBN 1-4034-5708-5 (Paperback)
1. Howe, Julia Ward, 1819-1910--Juvenile literature.
2. Authors, American--19th century--Biography--
Juvenile literature. 3. Feminists--United States--
Biography--Juvenile literature. [1. Howe,
Julia Ward, 1819-1910. 2. Authors, American. 3.
Feminists. 4. Women--Biography.] I. Title. II.
American lives (Heinemann Library
(Firm))
  PS2018.R38 2004
  811'.3--dc22
                        2003015752

Acknowledgments
The author and publishers are grateful to the
following for permission to reproduce copyright
material: Title page, pp. 13, 20, 22, 24, 25, 29
Bettmann/Corbis; pp. 4, 5, 10, 14, 15, 27 Reprinted
from *Julia Ward Howe*, Laura E. Richards and Maud
Howe Elliott, 1970; pp. 6, 17, 28 Library of Congress;
p. 7 Carmen Redondo/Corbis; p. 8 Redwood Library
and Athenaeum; p. 9 Corbis; p. 11 Courtesy National
Park Service; p. 12 www.haleysteele.com; p. 18
Hulton Archive/Getty Images; p. 19 Civil War
Photographs/Library of Congress; p. 21 Courtesy of
Cornell University Library, Making of America Digital
Collection. The Atlantic Monthly. Volume 9, Issue 52,
February 1862, p. 145; p. 23 Courtesy of the National
Register of Historic Places, photo by Robert C. Post
p. 26 Chicago Historical Society

Cover photograph by Hulton Archive/Getty Images

The author would like to thank Mary Smoyer,
President of the Board of Directors of the Boston
Women's Heritage Trail, for her assistance with
this project.

The publisher would like to thank Michelle Rimsa
for her comments in the preparation of this book.

Every effort has been made to contact copyright
holders of any material reproduced in this book.
Any omissions will be rectified in subsequent
printings if notice is given to the publisher.

The cover image of Julia Ward Howe was taken
around 1855. She was about 36 years old.

Contents

Some words are shown in bold, **like this.** You can find out what they mean by looking in the glossary.

Childhood

Julia Ward was born on May 27, 1819, in New York City. She was the fourth of seven children. Julia was especially close to her mother. When Julia was only five, her mother passed away.

Julia would always remember the happy times she spent with her mother, who was a poet. As a young girl, Julia read and wrote poems. When she grew up, her writing made her famous.

Julia was named after her mother, Julia Rush Ward. Mrs. Ward wrote poetry, but she never published it.

Julia's father hired **nannies** to care for the children after his wife's death. Julia was smart and had a lot of energy. She wanted to go to school and play outside like her big brothers.

Julia's father, Samuel Ward, was a successful banker.

But when Julia was a child, girls and boys led different lives. Boys wore sturdy clothes and boots when they played outside. Julia and her sisters wore fancy dresses and thin slippers. They were not allowed to play outdoors.

School

Teachers came to the Ward home to work with Julia and her sisters. Julia learned to speak French when she was very small. She had teachers for piano, dancing, and singing. Julia had a beautiful voice and loved to sing.

When Julia watched her brothers go off to **boarding school,** she was sad and jealous. She wanted to go to school, too, but her father wanted her to stay home and learn how to run a household.

When Julia was young, girls only went to school for a few years. They were expected to help out at home.

Julia loved learning. She spent a lot of time reading.

When Julia was nine, she was finally allowed to attend a private girls' school near her home. Julia had hoped to learn science and mathematics, but those subjects were thought to be too difficult for girls.

The next year, Julia attended a different school. There she studied Latin, Italian, and German. She read history, **philosophy,** and **chemistry** books.

Newport

Julia also wrote plays and poems. In 1832, when she was thirteen, she gave her father an entire book filled with the poems she had written. During that same year, all the Ward children caught **whooping cough.** Julia was sick for many weeks.

This is a painting of Julia and her older brothers, Samuel and Henry, from around 1825.

Whooping Cough

*Whooping cough is an infection of the lungs. People who have it make a whooping sound when they cough. In the 1830s there were no **antibiotics** to fight the disease. Before Julia was born, her three-year-old sister had died of whooping cough.*

When the children got better, Mr. Ward sent them to relatives in Newport, Rhode Island, for the summer. Newport was a small town on the Atlantic Ocean. Julia loved Newport. She raced along the beaches, grew healthy from eating fresh eggs and milk, and slept on mattresses filled with ground corn cobs.

Julia continued to visit Newport throughout her life. Visits to Newport always made her happy. Over the years, it became a popular summer **resort** for wealthy people.

This is the State House in Newport. It was built in 1832.

Poet

Julia finished school in 1835, when she was sixteen. She then studied history, geometry, and religion on her own. She also read books in French, German, Italian, and English. Julia's first poems were published in a magazine called *The American*.

This is a drawing of the Wards' home, called "The Corner," from around 1835.

Julia signed her poems "Anonymous," which meant that she did not want to give her name. Many people at the time thought women should not have **careers.** Julia's older brother Sam, however, encouraged her to write.

The Life of Julia Ward Howe

1819	1832	1843	1854	1861
Born in New York on May 27	*Spent first summer in Newport, Rhode Island*	*Married Dr. Samuel Gridley Howe*	*Published Passion Flowers*	*Wrote "B Hymn of Republic"*

When Sam married Emily Astor in 1838, Julia was in the wedding. She attended dinner parties and events at Sam and Emily's home. Julia loved to sing at parties and enjoyed being with Sam and Emily's friends.

However, her happiness ended when her father died in 1839. Her brother Henry died soon after, as well, adding to her sadness.

This is a drawing of Sam Ward, Julia's older brother.

Dr. Howe

In the summer of 1841, Julia was visiting friends in Boston. They invited her to tour the Perkins Institute, a famous school for the blind, and to meet the director, Dr. Samuel Gridley Howe. He was also a well-known doctor and teacher of the blind.

Dr. Howe was not in, but they found his student, ten-year-old Laura Bridgman in a classroom. Laura, the first deaf-blind person to attend school, was talking with another child by using sign language traced in her palm. Laura felt Julia Ward's face and told her she was pretty.

The Perkins Institute for the Blind was founded by Dr. Howe in 1832.

As they were about
to leave, a rider on
horseback galloped
across the meadow.
It was Dr. Howe.
He was handsome,
energetic, and fearless.
He had become a hero
when he fought with
the Greeks in a war
of **independence**
from Turkey.

Even though he was
eighteen years older
than Julia, she fell
in love with him.
Two years later,
on April 23, 1843,
they married.

Dr. Howe believed that blind
children could learn as much
as children who could see.
This picture of him was taken
many years after he met Julia.

Starting a Family

Dr. Howe and Julia, now called Mrs. Howe, traveled to Europe. Julia's sister, Annie, went with them. The Howes traveled to many countries, but spent the most time in Rome. It was there, in the spring of 1844, that their first child, Julia Romana, was born. While in Europe, they met many famous people. They met the writer Charles Dickens; Florence Nightingale, who later became a famous nurse; and many others.

Julia enjoyed traveling and meeting new people. This painting of her was done in 1847.

This was the Howe's home from 1846 to 1864. Some believe the house was named Green Peace because those were the first words Julia said upon seeing it.

After almost two years in Europe, the Howes returned to the United States. They moved to Boston and lived at the Perkins Institute. Julia did not like living at the school and dreamed of having a home of her own. When their second child was born in 1845, they named her after Florence Nightingale. In 1846 the family moved to a small house that Julia named Green Peace. It was a five-minute walk from the Perkins Institute.

A Book of Poems

Mrs. Howe's son Henry was born in 1848. Her daughter Laura was born in 1850. Mrs. Howe loved her children and her new home, but she missed her friends in New York. She liked writing poetry, but Dr. Howe felt that women should not be writers. In 1850 Mrs. Howe took her two youngest children to Rome, Italy. On the return trip, she wrote poetry. A few years later, she published the poems in a book called *Passion Flowers*.

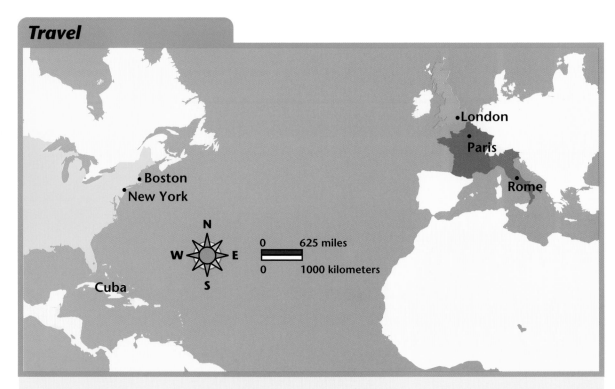

Travel

London

Paris

Rome

Boston
New York

N
W · E
S

0   625 miles

0   1000 kilometers

Cuba

Julia's trip to Europe inspired her to write more poetry.

Mrs. Howe's name did not appear in the book, but she sent copies to her friends. Soon everyone knew she was the author. Mrs. Howe received letters from famous poets who enjoyed her work.

Dr. Howe did not want his wife to have her own **career.** But despite his disapproval, Mrs. Howe kept writing. In 1854, the couple had another daughter, named Maud.

PASSION-FLOWERS.

BOSTON:
TICKNOR, REED, AND FIELDS.
M DCCC LIV.

Many copies of Julia's book of poetry were sold.

Julia Ward Firsts
- *First president of the American branch of the Women's International Peace Association*
- *First person to suggest a Mother's Peace Day*
- *First woman to become a member of the American Academy of Arts and Letters*

A Time of Change

In 1857 Mrs. Howe wrote another book of poetry and a play. On Christmas Day 1859, she gave birth to a baby boy. She named him Samuel, after his father. Dr. and Mrs. Howe now had six children. In 1860 she traveled to Cuba and wrote a book about her journey.

Her later books were not as **popular** as *Passion Flowers* had been, but Mrs. Howe kept writing. Several of her poems were published in the *Atlantic Monthly* magazine.

Julia's play *The World's Own* was performed in 1857 in New York and Boston theaters.

Soldiers lined up their cannons in Washington, D.C., ready to protect the city from Southern armies.

For several years, Dr. Howe and his friends had been working to end **slavery.** Mrs. Howe shared her husband's view that slavery was wrong. In previous years she had helped him with his **antislavery** newspaper, *Commonwealth*. But he did not want her to speak in public or to write about the **issue.** When the Civil War began in 1861, Dr. Howe offered to help the North, because he hoped the war would put an end to slavery. He went to Washington, D.C., and Mrs. Howe went with him.

A Powerful Song

In November 1861, Julia Ward Howe visited an army camp near Washington, D.C. The road was filled with marching soldiers. The Howes and their friends began to sing a popular song called "John Brown's Body." A friend traveling with them turned to Mrs. Howe and suggested that she write some new words to the song. That night she returned to the Willard Hotel in Washington and began writing.

This is a handwritten first draft of the "Battle Hymn of the Republic."

The words to the song were published in the *Atlantic Monthly*. It was an instant success. Soon soldiers were singing her song, "The Battle Hymn of the Republic," as they marched to war. It is said that when President Abraham Lincoln heard it sung, he cried.

People everywhere soon knew the name of the woman who had written "The Battle Hymn of the Republic." Everyone wanted to meet her and hear her speak.

THE

ATLANTIC MONTHLY.

A MAGAZINE OF LITERATURE, ART, AND POLITICS.

VOL. IX.—FEBRUARY, 1862.—NO. LII.

BATTLE HYMN OF THE REPUBLIC.

MINE eyes have seen the glory of the coming of the Lord :
He is trampling out the vintage where the grapes of wrath are stored ;
He hath loosed the fateful lightning of His terrible swift sword :
His truth is marching on.

I have seen Him in the watch-fires of a hundred circling camps ;
They have builded Him an altar in the evening dews and damps ;
I can read His righteous sentence by the dim and flaring lamps :
His day is marching on.

I have read a fiery gospel writ in burnished rows of steel :
"As ye deal with my contemners, so with you my grace shall deal ;
Let the Hero, born of woman, crush the serpent with his heel,
Since God is marching on."

He has sounded forth the trumpet that shall never call retreat ;
He is sifting out the hearts of men before His judgment-seat :
Oh, be swift, my soul, to answer Him ! be jubilant, my feet !
Our God is marching on.

In the beauty of the lilies Christ was born across the sea,
With a glory in his bosom that transfigures you and me :
As he died to make men holy, let us die to make men free,
While God is marching on.

Entered according to Act of Congress, in the year 1862, by TICKNOR AND FIELDS, in the Clerk's Office of the District Court of the District of Massachusetts.

VOL. IX.   10

Julia was paid $5 for printing her song. That would be about $100 in today's money.

Speaker and Women's Clubs

Dr. Howe agreed that Mrs. Howe could speak in public if she did not charge money. On January 1, 1863, she read "The Battle Hymn of the Republic" at a Boston event celebrating Lincoln's freeing of the slaves. As time went on, Julia found that she enjoyed public speaking. In 1865 her third poetry book, *Later Lyrics*, was published. Readers did not like it very much, though. People liked to hear her speak more than they liked to read her books.

Artist Winslow Homer created this illustration, titled "Songs of War" in 1861.

Times were changing. More women were attending schools and colleges. Women's clubs became another place to learn new skills and talk about important **issues.**

In May 1868, Mrs. Howe attended a meeting in Boston to form the New England Woman's Club. Many meetings were held at her Boston home. She enjoyed being with the smart, interesting women who took part in club activities.

The Julia Ward Howe house stands at 13 Chestnut Street in Boston.

Votes for Women

Julia Ward Howe came to believe that women should be allowed to vote and to have an equal say in making laws. In November, 1868, she gave a speech supporting women's **suffrage,** or right to vote.

In 1869 she helped form a nationwide group, the American Woman Suffrage **Association.** This group included both men and women. In 1870 Howe was elected president of the New England Woman Suffrage Association.

People who knew Howe saw her become a strong, determined person while discussing suffrage.

As she became more famous, Howe was asked to speak in public more often about her ideas.

For over 40 years, the Massachusetts **Legislature debated** women's suffrage. Howe attended these hearings and spoke in favor of women's suffrage. In 1870, she helped to begin the *Woman's Journal*, the most important suffrage magazine of the day. For twenty years, she worked as a writer and editor for the magazine.

Women's Suffrage

Women in the United States could not vote in national elections until 1920, when the Nineteenth Amendment to the Constitution was adopted.

Hoping for Peace

This picture is from a meeting of a women's group in 1909.

Howe also worked for peace. She hoped that women around the world would join together to prevent war. In 1871, she helped form the U.S. **branch** of the Women's **International** Peace **Association** and became its president. She preached about peace in churches, wrote about peace for magazines, and tried to organize an international peace conference. The conference never happened, so Howe came up with a new idea.

Howe's five children are shown here: Maud, Laura, Henry, Julia, and Florence.

Howe suggested that people celebrate Mothers' Peace Day every June 2. The first celebration was held on June 2, 1873, in Boston and seventeen other cities. It was a success, but it never happened again. Howe did not understand why Mothers' Peace Day did not continue. Today, many people believe that Howe's Mothers' Peace Day was the beginning of what we now call Mother's Day.

On January 9, 1876, Howe's husband died. She took some time away from her work to **mourn** his death.

Honors

Howe was 80 when she wrote her life story.

Howe preached in churches and spoke to large groups. She met presidents and world leaders. She was one of the most respected women of her time.

In 1899 Howe wrote *Reminiscences,* the story of her life. As she grew older, she gave fewer and fewer speeches, but when she did speak, people listened.

The little girl who had dreamed of going to school received **honorary** college degrees from Brown University and Smith College.

In January 1908, Howe was the first woman elected to the American Academy of Arts and Letters. This important award honored her work as a writer. She died two years later on October 17, 1910, in Newport, Rhode Island. She was 91.

Many famous people, including Clara Barton, founder of the American Red Cross, wrote **tributes** in praise of Julia Ward Howe. Hundreds of people attended her **funeral.** They honored her by singing "The Battle Hymn of the Republic."

Howe did many things to support other women. She was president of the Association for the Advancement of Women for nineteen years.

Glossary

antibiotics medicine that fights certain germs

antislavery against slavery

association organization of people with similar ideas

boarding school school that provides food and housing

branch part of a group or organization

career occupation or job

chemistry science that studies what things are made of and the changes they go through

debated argued about

funeral ceremony to honor a person who has died

honorary given as an honor

independence freedom

international including many nations

issue question to be discussed

legislature elected group of people who make the laws for a state

mourn to grieve or feel sorrow for someone who has died

nanny child's nurse or baby-sitter

philosophy study of ideas about knowledge and values

popular well-liked

reminiscence memory

resort place people go on vacation

slavery treating people as if they were property

suffrage right to vote

tribute praise

More Books to Read

Harness, Cheryl. *Remember the Ladies*. New York: HarperCollins, 2001.

Keller, Kristin Thoennes. *The Women Suffrage Movement, 1848-1920*. Mankato, Minn.: Bridgestone, 2003.

Pascoe, Elaine. *The Right to Vote*. Brooklyn, N.Y.: Millbrook Press, 1997.

Place to Visit

National Women's Hall of Fame
76 Fall Street
Seneca Falls, New York 13148
Visitor Information: (315) 568-8060

Index